bayaka

THE EXTRAORDINARY MUSIC OF **THE BABENZÉLÉ PYGMIES** AND SOUNDS OF THEIR FOREST HOME

Executive Producer Jeffrey Charno

Music by the Bayaka of Yandoumbé

Recordings & Text by Louis Sarno

Recordings Produced by Bernie Krause

Editor Stephen Ciabattoni

Art Direction/Design by *STAIN*

Photography by Louis Sarno & Yann Lussiez

ellipsis arts ⓐ ⓜ ⓢ

♻ Printed on recycled Paper in HK & bound in China By Palace Press International

FOR INFORMATION OR A CATALOG: ELLIPSIS ARTS...
20 LUMBER ROAD
ROSLYN, NY 11576
P: 516-621-2727 F: 516-621-2750
E-MAIL: ELLIARTS@AOL.COM

contents

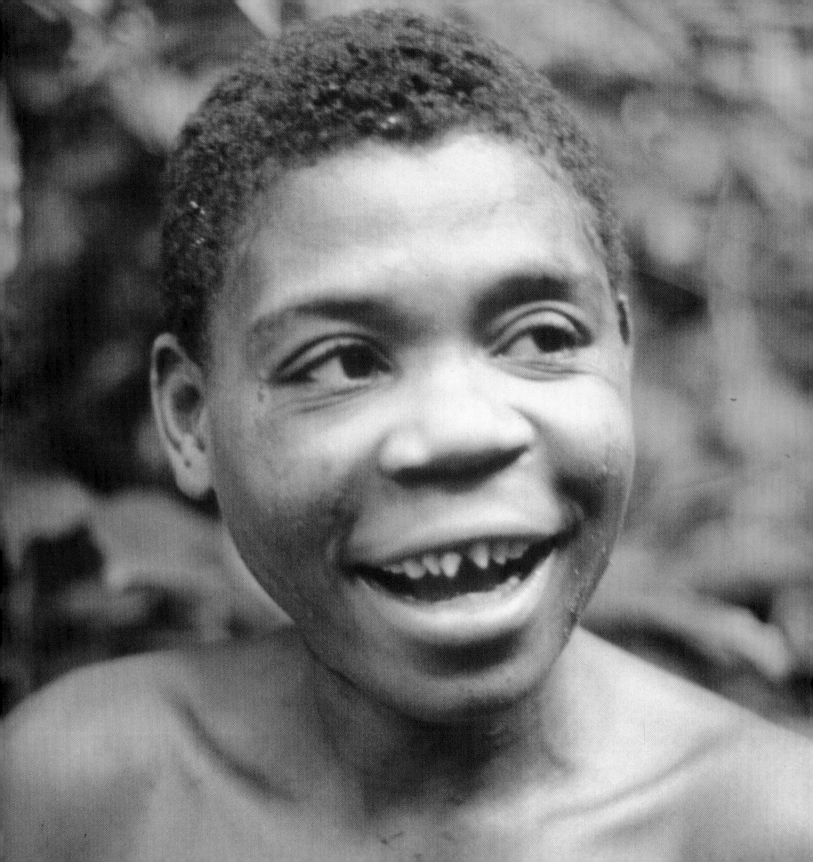

legacy and language

The Pygmies of central Africa are generally thought to comprise three main groups. In the Ituri forest of northeast Zaire live the people collectively known as Mbuti (i.e. Asua, Kango, Efé, etc.). Scattered throughout central Zaire are populations of Twa, who also inhabit the last forested patches of Rwanda. In the western Congo basin (i.e. west of the Ubangi river, including Congo, Central African Republic, Cameroon and Gabon) lies the third main group, sometimes referred to as BaMbenga. This group includes the Aka (between the Ubangi and Sangha rivers) and the Baka (west of the Sangha in southeast Cameroon all the way to northern Gabon), as well as smaller groups in central Gabon. Of these three main groups, recent research has determined that the Ituri forest Pygmies are genetically the farthest removed from other Africans, while the Twa are closer to the other Africans than they are to the Mbuti. The BaMbenga show closer genetic affinity with the Mbuti.

Within each main group of Pygmies are smaller clan divisions. BaNgombé is the easternmost clan of Baka. BaBenzélé (sometimes Ba-Benjelé or BaMbenzélé) is the easternmost clan of Aka. I live among the BaBenzélé. BaBenzélé refer to themselves, and to all Pygmy peoples (as opposed to other Africans), as Bayaka. This is a racial, not cultural, designation. It is also, by habit and preference, the name I use when discussing Pygmies.

The rain forest is an environment that swallows its own history. Few artifacts, few traces of ancient peoples, survive. It is known that in the past there was extensive migration throughout the forest by both Pygmies and Bantus, but the precise nature of those movements can only be conjectured. Currently it is believed that the Ituri forest was the original home of the Pygmies, and that a series of migrations eventually brought one group to the Western Congo Basin. The descendants of these western basin Pygmies are the Aka and Baka.

Language among the Bayaka is a complicated affair. Evidence exists to indicate there was once a single Bayaka language. This evidence consists mainly of certain words from the original language which have survived in usage to the present day. These words are unrelated to any known Bantu or Nilotic language. For example, the words *mboloko* (blue duiker, the most commonly caught animal on Bayaka net hunts) and *nkusa* (the vine from which rope for hunting nets is derived) are used by both the Aka west of the Ubangi and the Mbuti some eight hundred miles to the east, even though they speak totally different languages. This is also the case with many other specialized words, particularly (so I'm told) plant names. From such evidence researchers have postulated the existence of an original Bayaka language which was subsequently lost, leaving only tantalizing fragments. Today most Bayaka groups speak a version of the language of their Bantu or Nilotic neighbors. Some of these versions are apparently so idiosyncratic as to be virtually incomprehensible to outsiders. The BaBenzélé have taken this tendency to its logical extreme: they speak a Bantu language no longer spoken by anyone else. The Bantu from whom the language derived presumably either went extinct, or were assimilated by other groups.

There has been considerable speculation about how the Bayaka throughout Africa came to lose their language. Language is one facet of culture that dies hard. Unassimilated minority populations usually hold fast to their language, even in the face of severe adversity – witness the Basques and the Kurds. In addition, some groups that have been assimilated into a larger, dominant society still cling to their own language. How is it then, that the Bayaka – who have neither been assimilated nor been the victims of systematic persecution – seem to have lost their language centuries ago? In most places Bayaka traditional life remains strong and vibrant. The disappearance of their language is a paradox.

yandoumbé

Today I live in a BaBenzélé village called Yandoumbé. I helped to found this village in December 1990. Yandoumbé is by no means a "traditional" Bayaka settlement. For one thing, it is far too big. In a traditional roadside settlement, one normally finds between fifteen to seventy-five people. Yandoumbé has well over two hundred souls, comprising five or six extended families. Even these extended families are related through numerous intermarriages. Yandoumbé is the largest all-Bayaka community within the confines of the Dzanga-Sangha Dense Forest Reserve (the extreme southwest tip of the Central African Republic), but it is not the largest Bayaka community in the region. Some forty miles to the north, in the savanna bordering the forest, lies Monasao, a Bayaka village founded in the mid-seventies by a Catholic priest. Monasao's population now exceeds fifteen hundred.

When we founded Yandoumbé, leaving our old mosquito-ridden site between the town and the sawmill, moving up the hill out of the Sangha Valley, the Bayaka made a conscious decision to follow the example of Monasao. Under the guidance of their priest, the Bayaka at Monasao had cultivated large fields of manioc (a versatile, edible tuber) and, freed from their major dependence on the villagers (non-Bayaka) for this daily staple, had become economically independent. Monasao had an infirmary where medical problems were treated, a shop for Bayaka only with subsidized prices, and a government-recognized school where the children learned to read and write. The major flaw in the Monasao set-up was that the Bayaka had

merely traded, to a large degree, economic dependence on the villagers for economic dependence on the Catholic church. There could be no doubt, however, that they were in many ways better off than Bayaka who still depended, and lived in conjunction with, the villagers.

The Bayaka at Yandoumbé decided to have a go at creating a Monasao-like community, but without the Catholic church (they had little enthusiasm for the Monasao Sunday service at which everyone sang songs about Jesus with what the Bayaka considered simple harmonies compared to their sophisticated musical inventions.) They would all cultivate manioc plantations. Never again would they have to barter for manioc from the villagers. And one day, they declared, Yandoumbé would have its own school, its own infirmary, and maybe even a shop with subsidized prices.

Within a year Yandoumbé was practically self-sufficient in the production of manioc. When during one season elephants destroyed many of the manioc plantations of the villagers from the nearby town, the desperate villagers turned to the Bayaka, who had enough of a manioc surplus to sell some to them. It was a historic reversal of roles.

Yandoumbé is a unique and extraordinary village, and even on the most uneventful days my sense of wonder at being there is never far from the surface. Yandoumbé is no Monasao. For one thing, squeezed into a small cleared area next to the road and hemmed in by forest, Yandoumbé has the population density of a town rather than a village, and usually has the frenetic energy to match. At Monasao, with its open savanna spaces and four-mile extent along both sides of the road, the Bayaka have scattered their homes in little groups isolated and often hidden from one another by tall grasses. There is always an atmosphere of self-contained calm at Manasao. The central authority of the priest and his assistants has imposed a kind of order over community life. Most of the Bayaka work on projects that are, in effect, commissioned by the Catholic church.

Yandoumbé has no such luxury. Although by cultivating manioc fields the Bayaka have definitely improved their economic lot, daily life still compels them to constantly deal with the world beyond their own community. The traditional Bayaka/villager relationship which prevailed here as in other parts of Africa, whereby Bayaka families were "owned" over generations by villager families, began to break down locally in the early seventies with the opening of the sawmill. At the time many Bayaka (particularly those who later founded Yandoumbé) took the opportunity to break away from the villagers and work directly for the Yugoslavian-owned logging company. The founding of Yandoumbé was the final act in this break. It is a Bayaka community of free agents, and today in their many transactions with the outside world – be it as providers of a service, as employees, as traders, as consumers – the Bayaka maintain a high degree of independence and choice. Their many interactions with the outside world give Yandoumbé a busy air.

The Bayaka tend to have an irreverent attitude toward any form of central authority. Traditionally they lived without chiefs, and their own society verges on anarchy. In small forest communities such anarchy and the individual freedom it allows is balanced by a strong bond of cooperation as everyone busies themselves for the common good. In a large community by the road, such as Yandoumbé, these anarchistic tendencies can become self-destructive. Yandoumbé has grown up without a genuine authority figure and is like a creature without a head. At any moment it is ready to self-destruct, to negate itself, and in fact is continually doing so. Intrigues, feuds, disputes, jealousies and schemes (all the elements of life in a large community) are resolved, dissolved or at least temporarily deferred by the Bayaka's high mobility. They are always moving house. I have seen a single argument result in one family abandoning their big new bamboo house, still under construction but nearly finished, in order to move to the far side of Yandoumbé. These villager-style bamboo houses with palm thatching and mud-plastered walls are what the Bayaka prefer to live in along the road, as opposed to the leaf huts they still make in forest camps. Yandoumbé bustles with construction activity. There are also whole miniature neighborhoods which, suddenly abandoned, are either demolished by their former residents, or else allowed to crumble slowly through the forces of nature. Occasionally, new arrivals take up residence in one of these derelict houses, until they can arrange better accommodation. Life at times resembles a game of musical houses. I myself have lived in four different homes so far.

With Yandoumbé the Bayaka have created a kind of interface between their forest world and the money economy which prevails beyond the edge of the forest. The pressures and temptations to join this economy, to compete in the world on its terms, are tremendous and increasing daily. In their exchanges with the outside world, the Bayaka crave the respect due to them as human beings, but all too often denied them because the villagers view them as similar to the animals, living and dying in the forest. As part of their effort to prove the villagers wrong, the Bayaka (especially the men) often seek paid work, of which in the Dzanga-Sangha region there are now many possibilities. Some men take jobs as tree prospectors for the resurrected logging company; a few find temp work with the World Wildlife Fund which helps coordinate the conservation project there; still others may accept (illegal) hunting commissions from one of the villagers (usually a local official) who owns a gun. The list is long. With their wages they buy the clothes necessary for their interactions with the villagers. Any man who visits the nearby town without a shirt is arrested and fined.

Everyone at Yandoumbé already has a minimum base level of wealth because of their manioc plantations. Some individuals or couples spend more time augmenting this wealth than others. But village life brings with it more insidious influences too: appetites for alcohol and tobacco, to which the men are especially prone, and on which they invariably squander some of their hard-earned cash. These are not influences that one can legislate against for the Bayaka's protection, but rather temptations which the Bayaka themselves must learn to meet responsibly.

From Yandoumbé's beginning I have watched these hunter-gatherers tackle the challenge of creating a genuine village from scratch. Sometimes I think I am witnessing the future of the Bayaka, that Yandoumbé is in the vanguard of the kind of acculturation we can expect to see happening eventually to Bayaka communities everywhere. This bizarre mix of Bayaka anarchy and brilliant mimicry of villager civilization results in some startling and incongruous scenes, at times verging on a theater of the preposterous. To all appearances this seems to be the life the Bayaka are choosing for themselves. Perhaps they are simply making the best of necessity.

The days go by, and I watch as the Bayaka's entanglements with the outside world grow ever more complicated and problematic. For a while I am bemused. But as a week, and then two, slip by without a significant traditional dance, and the chaos and noise mount, and the teenagers do their best to dress like they were auditioning for *Saturday Night Fever* and dance to highlife (a form of pop music from Zaire) songs on the radio, I turn into a reactionary old crank. I sit with the elders and we complain: what's become of this younger generation? I lecture the kids: do you realize what you're giving up? Most of them have grown up knowing me and laugh at my old-fashioned ideas. "Hey," they say in so many words, "this is now!"

And then, just as I despairingly conclude that the tradition of large collective ceremonies has died at Yandoumbé, that the forest spirits will become mere phantoms of memory, the crazy free-for-all energy that makes Yandoumbé a contradiction of itself suddenly focuses into one irresistible force as those very teenagers who last night were disco champions now pound out traditional polyrhythms on the drums. Petty disputes are suspended, discord melts away. Almost before I realize, a dance is underway. Soon the whole community is together, and the inspiration of the singing transports everyone into a world where magic is real. The town, the road, nothing exists anymore except the music and the dancing of the spirits. These are the moments when I remember not only why I came here in the first place, but also why I remain.

a lifeline in song

Bayaka music is one of the hidden glories of humanity. From the Gabon coast practically all the way to the Rift Valley in the east, this music has a recognizable quality, with an emphasis on full, rich voice and bright-sounding pentatonic (five-note scale) harmonies. Nevertheless, stylistic differences among the various groups exist. At Yandoumbé I played tapes for the residents (predominantly BaBenzélé). Simha Arom's recordings from the sixties of the BaBenzélé in the savanna to the north, where Monasao now is, had the most immediate appeal. I had never before heard the *hindewhu* (papaya whistle) at Yandoumbé, but when I played Arom's recordings of this instrument, the Bayaka immediately recognized it and for several days made their own and played them. Other music with which they found affinity was that of the Baka Bambouké in northern Gabon, the BaNgombé in Cameroon and the Aka at Mongoumbé along the Ubangi River. Songs from all of these groups have entered Yandoumbé's vast repertoire. Music from the Mbuti of the Ituri forest (Efé, Sua, Kango, etc.) was the most difficult for Yandoumbé to relate to. Some of it made them laugh, some of it genuinely shocked them with its "wrong" harmonies. The children, however, were fascinated, and for days after they imitated these harmonies, albeit with exaggerated dissonance.

Why are the Bayaka so musical? Living with them, I see part of the answer all around me. Children grow up in the midst of music. As babies they are serenaded constantly with lullabies, often sung by both parents or a parent and an older sibling. They snuggle in the laps of their mothers during dance ceremonies, when the decibel level rattles eardrums, and hang on when their mothers leap to their feet and dance. Babies rarely cry during these all-night events. So total is their immersion in music, that in the same formative years during which language acquisition takes place and the brain is still physically growing, Bayaka children also acquire a complete innate knowledge of the "rules" of their music. The ability to create melodies and harmonize is as deeply automatic and universal to the Bayaka as is the average person's ability to speak sentences in his or her native language. Musically speaking, the Bayaka all begin life as child prodigies.

There is no musician class in Bayaka society, just as there is no chief or shaman class. The well-known griot tradition of West Africa, in which music has become an occupational specialty and even a matter for heredity, simply does not exist among the Bayaka. Individual talent, however, differs from person to person, and when it is outstanding it is recognized and appreciated. At Yandoumbé, for example, Balonyona is considered the supreme player of the *geedal* (bow-harp) although many men and boys also play the instrument with talent. Momboli, or Contreboeuf as he prefers to be known, is a great *mbyo* (notched flute) virtuoso. Certain teenage boys gain popularity for their drumming skills. Men like Mobo and Gondo and Tabu have earned renown as storytellers. These various masteries are largely a matter of choice. Children teach themselves to play instruments. After singing (which Bayaka children begin to do almost before they can talk) drumming is the earliest musical activity practiced while they are still toddlers. Boys pluck their first exploratory tunes on the *geedal* around the age of seven. The *mondumé* (harp-zither) is not taken up seriously until adulthood, while the *mbyo* is only played these days by a few older men.

The girls and women do not as a rule play instruments, so from earliest infancy their musical education and development primarily concerns their voices. Whenever those precocious four-year-old boys are drumming away on a battery of plastic jerrycans and tin bowls, you can be sure to find equally precocious four-year-old girls singing nearby. From what they attempt, it's clear they already know the ground rules for improvisation, they just don't have the technical ability yet to execute it properly. By the time they are teenagers they have the technical ability, and the genius, to sing music that sends shivers down the spine. At middle age their music has the power to heal damaged souls. Certain older women may gain local renown as talented mime artists who dance out the stories in sung fables called *gano*; others become master storytellers, telling long stories alive with the voices of a dozen characters and interspersed with songs. These epics take place in a mythic long ago and are embellished without any qualms whatsoever with all sorts of anachronisms (the chimpanzee that steals the first fire for humans wears army boots; the original tree hyrax listens to a radio). These tales can take up half the night. They are always riveting.

Exploration and experimentation with sound is a typical Bayaka trait. They are acoustic rather than visual people, a bias that makes sense in the rain forest, where some birds you hear all your life may never show themselves once. Their curiosity about sound and their natural musical invention have resulted in some unusual and wonderful music, such as their justifiably famous *koondi* (water drum), where bathing girls cup their hands and slap the water, causing a deep percussive sound that may carry for more than a mile. The tone of the water can even be roughly controlled. The girls can get some complicated rhythms going, yodeling lovely melodies in accompaniment. Some species of trees have buttress roots which give a loud resonating thump when struck. If such a tree happens to stand along a trail, boys and girls always rap a brief tattoo on it when passing by. Chimpanzees drum on these trees when they find them, too. Long ago, probably generations already, some Bayaka (of the BaBenzélé clan) discovered an "earth drum," a unique piece of ground which resonates profoundly as one walks across it. Knowledge of this place of special sound deep in the forest has been passed down to the present day. Many Bayaka have been there, and a great many more know of it through word of mouth.

As regards percussion, the Bayaka have an eminently practical attitude. They love the powerful throb of the large duiker-skin drums, but if these aren't available they can make due with whatever is at hand. The combination of big aluminum pots and plastic jerrycans is the favorite substitution, and the boys can pump out some extraordinary sounds with them. One interesting fact is that no percussion ensemble is considered complete without at least one piece of metal to tap. Whether it be a section of corrugated tin, a machete blade or an aluminum bowl, the Bayaka like the sharp sound of metal. For some reason this predilection has always made me think of the Bayaka's need for iron. The acquisition of iron for use must have been a major event in Bayaka history, and I see their insistence on metal in the percussion line-up as symbolic of this historic moment. A far greater restraint characterizes their use of glass bottles for percussion. It is notably absent from many of the big ceremonies but frequently used in sung fables. Its bright sound is always sought to complement the delicate tones of the *mondumé*.

The children are always making toy instruments: from scraps of cellophane they devise kazoos; the hollow leaf stems of papayas can be turned into tooters; grass stalks played properly make the raucous noise of New Year's party blowers. Once at Yandoumbé a couple of men showed me an instrument I'd never seen before: a long piece of rattan was tied around one of the support poles of a house. It was then tied to a stick and pulled tautly across the open top of a large aluminum pot. The other man drummed on the rattan with two sticks while his partner altered the tension of the rattan, thereby raising or lowering its tone. The staccato speed of the main rhythm, combined with the wild fuzzy rattle of the pot as it resonated and vibrated, and the notes of the rattan itself as they rose or fell sharply in reckless glissandos, made for a truly bizarre, electronic sound. They called this oddball hybrid a *boolaboo*. The seven-year-old boys took note. After that single performance by the two men, children everywhere began making and playing *boolaboos,* until Yandoumbé was positively buzzing with *boolaboos.* For their purposes, the boys used any pots they could get their hands on, and any bit of exposed pole (such as the wall of a house) was fair game as an anchor for their rattan. Women were always chasing them away and reclaiming pots. Men who were trying to nap, an enterprise doomed as soon as a *boolaboo* began to throb like some didjeridoo gone amok within inches of their heads, would confiscate the children's rattan, and threaten spankings if they were disturbed again. But like guerrilla action the *boolaboos* kept springing up; highly mobile units of three children each, now both boys and girls, kept up a steady action. I was the only homeowner who didn't chase them away and so my house became a sort of base of operations. Sometimes three *boolaboos* would be going at once. A couple of times they were so loud and reverberating (I could feel my whole house shaking) that my neighbors were provoked to make a request unheard of among the Bayaka: they asked me to keep the music down.

That was a couple of years ago already, and *boolaboo* fever has since subsided. Occasionally some of the veterans of that campaign (little Elivé, now nine; ten-year-old Malala; the two Ayoosis) get together and jam, but they've already turned their real interest to more serious instruments: drums and the *geedal*.

Recently the first generic guitar has made an appearance at Yandoumbé. A young man named Ngongo Joseph carved a light wood into the shape of an electric guitar and equipped it with several nylon strings. He has been teaching himself to play it and has already composed his first song ("Yandoumbé Has Won"), in a gentle highlife style. It is telling that this new-fangled instrument should be introduced by one of the few Yandoumbé residents who can read and write. Since he was a teenager Ngongo has worked for the World Wildlife Fund in their health program, and been taught basic literacy. Although his father Mobila is a gifted musician on both harp-zither and flute, Ngongo himself only knows how to play his homemade guitar. He participates in *elanda* (young people's dance) and other large musical events, but he is firmly of the new generation, with one foot maintaining a toe hold on the forest and the other inching cautiously towards the contemporary world.

Yandoumbé is a dynamic community encompassing two worlds. Nothing illustrates this better than those times when, at the end of some ceremony, the teenagers have sought out a working cassette player and started to dance to highlife songs. Since on these occasions I have just had ample proof of the teenagers' formidable talents for their traditional music and dance, I cannot accuse them of ignoring tradition. Privately, however, I wonder how much longer this tradition will interest them. Is Ngongo's guitar, however endearing and quaint, a symptom of the beginning of the end?

Whenever such thoughts depress me, I know I must get away – into the cool and peace and deep shade of the forest.

the orchestra

Above all, it's to the sounds of the forest that I tune, not merely my ears, but my entire being. There are many levels of sound. The most basic, the electronic pulse which never ceases, is composed of legions of tireless insects – the crickets, katydids and their kin. Special mention must be made of the awesome white noise of the cicadas. These sleek insects are notorious noisemakers. Two thousand years ago Virgil complained of cicadas that "they burst the very shrubbery with their noise." Legend has it that in the nineteenth century the great explorer-scientist Humboldt set up a cannon beneath one raucous specimen and had it fired several times, with no dissuasive effect on the cicada's din whatsoever. More than once I've been in the midst of a delicate recording, some long sought-after sound such as the rising song of the red-chested cuckoo sung by several birds at the same time, or the gentle vocalizations of a large family of colubus monkeys feeding and relaxing in the canopy above, when a single cicada has suddenly decided to advertise itself to the opposite sex and blasted its burst of white noise directly into my microphones, sending the recording level into overload. More than once, too, I've abandoned my microphones to pursue the guilty cicada, chasing it from tree trunk to tree trunk, full of rage and grimly determined to destroy the insect with my projectiles of sticks and baseball-sized fruits. On one of my hot-headed pursuits the cicada led me so far afield that afterwards it took me an hour to relocate my recorder. And yet, in fact, no sound is more evocative of the forest, and when the Bayaka hear the voice of the *élélé* (cicada), they say it makes their hearts glad.

To the rasps, chirps, whirs and clicks of the Orthoptera and Homoptera must be added the steady hum of the Diptera, Hymenoptera and Coleoptera – the fly, bee and beetle kingdoms. They buzz in the air absolutely everywhere. Taken together in their trillions they produce an omnipresent, slightly oscillating hum.

On the next level are the twitters, peeps, warbles, coos and chirrups of the little birds – the bulbuls, shrikes, trogons, cuckoos, orioles, doves and many others. These are sounds that come and go but seldom are completely absent. Sometimes, on the other hand, they occur in such density or in conjunction with so many other sounds as to constitute a major sound event. One delightful feature of the tropical rain forest is that parties of birds of many different species often feed together. Their arrival can transform an area from almost total silence into an orchestra of bird song.

Then there are the larger birds and many of the mammals. Their voices are so distinctive that close up they always strongly mark the moment of their occurrence, distinguishing it from the moments before and after. The gobbling call of nearby blue turaco is an extraordinary sound by itself, but when it triggers a response from all the blue turacos in the vicinity it is a truly memorable event, the kind I'm ever on the prowl to record.

Certain voices of the forest are so elusive, so unpredictable, that their capture on tape has become a kind of holy grail for me: 1) The deep, motorboat putt-putt of a goliath beetle in flight. This massive insect is possibly the world's heaviest, and in flight it resembles a brown-and white baseball, wobbling clumsily in ever-widening circles until, having gained sufficient momentum, it bumbles off. 2) The nocturnal call of the *kimbi,* or pygmy rail, a veritable one-bird orchestra that skulks in the marshes. Small, brown and inconspicuous, the *kimbi* is rarely seen, but its voice carries a long way – a deep "hu-hu" delivered in a distinctive rhythm and seemingly accompanied by drums and horns. 3) A passing bee swarm. Honeybees are a major presence in the rain forest and a force to be reckoned with. Nothing gives so clear a picture of the awesome potential as the sound of an entire hive swarming past above the canopy, a hum that seems to subsist in, and then to gently detach itself from, the background noise of the forest. The hum mutates gradually into the rush of a steady breeze, then into a roar, a distressing chord made up of countless microtones amplified fifty thousand times, a doomsday buzz from another dimension that can short-circuit one's brain with fear. It swells to a frightening crescendo, the flight paths of individual bees become audible, one wants to run, to get the hell out of there. A few seconds later the crescendo loses its power and the roar begins to recede, soon only a hum dying away, reabsorbed into the perpetual thrum of the forest.

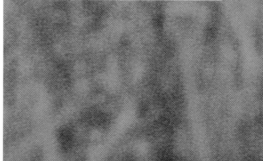

Some animal sounds (chimpanzees, gorillas, elephants) are worth recording at every opportunity simply because the animals themselves are a source of fascination and no two vocalizations are ever alike. Their utterances add something profound and moving to the sonic texture of the forest, a reminder of other, non-human consciousness that dwells in this world of deep shade.

run into the forest

Yandoumbé is such a large community that at almost any time of the year there is bound to be at least one group (often several) off in the forest somewhere. These forest camps vary in size from one or two households to twenty-five. The large camps invariably are net-hunting camps, the smaller ones usually for gathering *payu* (a forest seed used in sauces). These latter support themselves most often with the occasional animal killed by crossbow. Men, women and children all participate in these forest sojourns. Camps rarely remain in one place for more than a month. Occasionally, a troupe of only men will depart on *esendo*, a walkabout in the forest with spears in search of large game (nowadays almost exclusively bushpig, in former times also elephant and gorilla). These excursions last from ten to thirty days, and the men rarely sleep in the same place more than two nights in a row.

When I want to join a forest camp, I pack my recording equipment and notebooks, stock up on instant coffee, organize a supply of manioc for myself (these days I buy it from the Bayaka), and set off. Sometimes a single teenage guide accompanies me, sometimes several families who are heading for the same camp.

My first thought on entering the forest is always the same: why haven't I done this before? I find myself wondering how those I've left behind can tolerate staying in the village. That's not to say that Yandoumbé doesn't have its moments. I think back on ceremonies (*ejengi, boyobi, limboku, so*) that I have witnessed there. I remember the utter dependability of Contreboeuf's nightly rise at three in the morning to serenade our quiet village with his flute, and know that for a few days at least I will miss his melodies. I smile when I recall evenings of musical games by the children, or the night the boys challenged the girls to tug-of-war, and lost five times in a row! These contests are worth describing.

A thick vine about seventy-five feet long (or more likely two vines tied together) is laid along the ground. At its midpoint two opponents face each other and sit down. With shouts of bravado and taunts against each other, more and more people choose sides and line up behind the two leaders. Teams quickly form of thirty or more per side. Sitting down, everybody picks up their section of vine. Then they sing a kind of musical round while they rock backwards and forwards in unison like rowers. As excitement mounts they stand up, then someone cries "Get ready, get set..." and the singing stops as the two teams lock in battle. A team wins when they overcome their opponents and pull them forward one and all until they fall. Just as often the vine snaps, and both teams go flying backwards and land on their behinds. I love the songs that accompany these games. They are delightful little rounds that remind me of children singing and playing "Row, row, row your boat."

As we move along the forest trails my mind dwells a little longer on Yandoumbé; I think fondly about those who've stayed behind, their waves and salutations as I left, and the way they called out, "I'm coming in two days!" "We'll meet you at the Makupa River in a week!" "Save me some honey! I'll be out tomorrow!" Some of them really will come, others will remain by the road after all, to go out another time.

Soon the sheer beauty of the forest empties my mind of memories and musings and awakens me to the present moment. Now my senses feast on the complex mosaic of impressions that come at me from all directions. Tropical forests are places where biodiversity has peaked, perhaps even reached its saturation point. Life exists on all levels, no niche is left unexplored, no resource unexploited. I pause to examine the corpse of a large black ant, a mere exoskeleton now, like the wreck of a tank, frozen in mid-stride upon the stalk of some plant, where it finally succumbed to the parasitic fungus that had been consuming it from the inside and that now grows out of the corpse: teensy toadstools on hair-thin stalks. These toadstools themselves have become parasatized by a furry white mold which in turn provides a whole world for some incredibly tiny mites. Farther on I stop to marvel at an especially large tree. These forest giants are worlds unto themselves, with their immense boughs spreading out and draped in miniature forests of epiphytes. Orchids, ferns and mosses support a rich variety of life, from shrubs and even young trees whose roots find nutrients and take hold in the layers of vegetation already there, to thriving pondlife communities in the pools of water trapped by the vegetation and treeholes. Only slightly less breathtaking to me are the huge lianas. Thicker than a human torso, they lunge in and out of the earth like the humps of sea serpents, twisting and coiling and folding in upon themselves before tapering into giant

cables that stretch up into the canopy and across the trees, only to descend to earth again somewhere farther along, where they shoot out more roots and swell into pythons. With so many established root centers, a single giant liana has considerable guarantees against accidental mortality.

The forest floor itself always holds my fascination. The canopy is too high, and often obscured from view as well, for a ground observer to make out the shapes of most leaves, or whether a tree is in flower or fruit. But the forest floor reveals much: pods and fruits and blossoms litter the ground, providing a catalogue of tree and liana species in a given area. Sometimes the fragrance in the air changes every twenty feet from the fermented tang of overripe and rotting yellow fruits to the jasmine-like perfume of a recent fall of white starfish blossoms to the old-socks smell of large moldy seeds that failed to germinate.

Forest life is an altogether different proposition from life in the village. On a basic level the forest represents simple escape. Since time immemorial, I have no doubt, many a Moaka (the singular of Bayaka) have resorted to flight into its vast tangled interior to avoid the consequences of an unpaid debt or a transgression of law. Even I've had recourse to the forest in this capacity. Sometimes the Bayaka use the phrase "run into the forest" as a euphemism for "escape."

In the forest the whole social agenda is utterly changed. All the conflicts that necessarily arise when a group of hunter-gatherers tries to mesh its existence with 20th century town life literally get left behind. Problems of civic duty, the pros and cons of formal education, the exploitation of labor, the prejudices, the complicated dynamics of diverse populations in contact and often at odds with one another (Bayaka, villager, expatriate), the dangerous undertow of the cash economy are the factors that handicapped the Bayaka in their everyday village life. There, even the simplest exchange or act is never really simple containing the seeds of all these dilemmas. In the forest, this tiresome burden to existence is left back in the village like a sack of hot potatoes. Certainly this is one reason for the tremendous feeling of liberation every time we move into the forest. Each one of us has problems we've left unresolved, but these will begin to fade in importance, and then even from memory. Stay in the forest long enough, and the whole rest of the world will start to fade away.

The problems that remain are mostly logistic: how far to go, what time to stop, where to camp, what to eat. In the forest, the women really come into their own. Sidelined in the modern economy of town life, as soon as they step into the forest they regain their traditional status and the political clout that goes with it. As a rule the women neither smoke nor drink, so it is always frustrating for them in the village to watch their men squander hard-earned francs on those "bad foods," as the women call both tobacco and alcohol. There will be no more of that.

Everyone who has spent time with the Bayaka both in village and forest has remarked on the extraordinary differences in behavior (exhibited by the men in particular) in the two worlds. More than one anthropologist has used the word "schizo-phrenic" to describe the change. This is accurate if by schizophrenic they mean "split personality," for many of the men really do seem to have two distinct personalities, almost as if this was the method they evolved to accommodate the extremes of personality they have had to adopt for dealing with the world. Some people roll both good and bad all into one personality. The Bayaka men prefer to separate them into two, one which they assume in the village, and the other which they reserve for the forest. One cannot usually predict the forest man from knowing only the village man. This is even more true the other way around. One immediate conclusion to be drawn from this: take away the forest from the Bayaka, and the men especially will lose access to that which makes them complete beings. For most of them, their forest personalities will vanish with the trees.

Stay in the forest long enough and

the whole rest of the world will start to fade away

Climatically, the rain forest is a different world from the road. Even at the height of the dry season, for instance, when for weeks without relief the village bakes in the undiluted fury of the tropical sun, there are thunderstorms deep in the forest. To my mind there's just no comparison: the forest is cool and shady, filled with the most marvelous, sweet sounds, teeming with a mostly hidden wildlife including our closest relatives, the chimpanzees and gorillas, a kingdom where plants and especially trees reign supreme, where life takes on some of its seemingly most gratuitously beautiful forms. Daytime inconveniences (persistently inquisitive honeybees, ubiquitous *melipones,* or sweat bees, that love nothing more than to crawl into your eyes or nose, and biting flies of various kinds) tend to be rather moderate and more than made up for by the profound tranquillity of the nights, when in contrast to the village there are no mosquitoes. Sleep becomes a kind of bliss, one is floated gently through the oxygen-rich night on a current of pulsating nocturnal sounds.

The Bayaka know the forest intimately, and have favorite areas for making camps. Some places have probably been camped in for generations, but after five years not a trace remains of even the largest camp. Recently I was walking with a small party through very closed forest when we emerged in a stretch of bimba forest (areas dominated by bimba, or *Gilbertiodendron*, trees). The place was so breathtakingly spacious, the air so green and fragrant with bimba blossoms, which were dropping to the ground everywhere like big pink snowflakes, that I asked to pause for a moment so I could take it all in. I was amazed when my companions told me that we were standing in our old Sao-Sao camp from 1989. I couldn't see a hint of it. I questioned them: Where was my hut? Where was the *mbanjo* (men's shelter)? They remembered everything, and pointed out all the spots, now completely reverted to forest.

During the short dry season, when storms are less likely to occur, the Bayaka prefer to make camp in bimba forest. The problem with the bimba tree, however, is that it is very fragile, branches are constantly snapping off in the wind; after a rainfall whole trees come crashing to the ground. This fragility helps bimba trees shed any ambitious lianas, and consequently bimba forest is very open and light, almost like a temperate sycamore forest. However, camping in bimba is risky business even at the best of times. If storms are at all likely to occur, the Bayaka opt for a spot in the more closed mixed forest, preferably without any wonky-looking big trees.

Sometimes they have arguments about the merits of different locations, while to me both places look equally unpromising, dense with undergrowth. Once they decide, everyone gets to work. The men and boys tackle the undergrowth with machetes and homemade axes; the women and girls clear the ground of leaf litter and debris, scraping away until they reach the humus beneath the surface layer of mulch. Meanwhile the small children play. The attack on the forest may appear random, but in fact the Bayaka have the capacity to envision in advance exactly how a finished camp will look. What at first seems like a haphazard arrangement of hut sites turns out, as the underbrush is cleared away and the shape of the camp emerges, to be roughly a circle. In very large encampments, the classic circle arrangement is retained, but instead of single huts around the circumference one finds clusters of huts based on family affiliation. Each of these family clusters has its own sometimes tiny central space where the "neighborhood" children may hold little dances. Larger events take place in the main central clearing.

Every camp has a *mbanjo*, a clubhouse-sleeping shelter for bachelors, widowers, visitors without wives, and teenage boys. The *mbanjo* usually stands in the central clearing, off to one side. For young teenage boys in particular the *mbanjo* makes an important change in their way of life from the village, where most of them sleep in the big bamboo houses of their parents. In the forest they form an independent unit, are responsible for constructing the *mbanjo* themselves, and to an extent fend for themselves as far as food is concerned. Beds are platforms of poles raised a few inches above the ground. Many a time I have visited camps and slept in their *mbanjos*. Sometimes their beds are one extensive platform on which everyone stakes a position; others beds have several narrow pole benches. In either case I've always been amazed at how many boys can fit themselves onto these platforms when they want to sleep. This is not to say that they are necessarily comfortable. The night is frequently marked by minor tussles as boys vie for space or try to rearrange somebody else's intruding elbow or foot. Occasionally, one hears the dull thud of someone falling onto the ground.

The construction of the big bamboo houses in the village is men's work, and depending on the effort put into it a house might take months to build. In the forest, house-making is the work of women (except the *mbanjo*), and in as little time as two hours they can throw the basic structure up. They use skinny supple poles, which are stuck into the ground about five or six feet apart and then bent over into an arch and entwined together. Once a hemispherical, or beehive-shaped, space has been enclosed, the women weave and tie crosspoles through the framework to create a kind of lattice. This lattice they then tile over with large oval *ngungu (Megaphrynium)* leaves, starting at the bottom and working up to the apex. A carefully made hut with fresh *ngungu* leaves can withstand the most torrential downpours, with not a drop entering from above. However, the contour of the ground frequently results in rivulets flowing through the huts, and little trenches redirecting the flow are always necessary. Those with foresight dig trenches around their huts in advance; others wait until the storm is upon them, then do it during the heaviest part of the rain, usually in the pitch dark. After huts are leafed over with ngungu, the women cover the huts with leafy branches as an extra protection; with such a covering the huts blend into the forest background perfectly, looking like nothing but humps of tangled vegetation.

In many places in the forest *ngungu* leaves don't grow. Then women use some less effective substitute, and top this substitute with a large strip of bimba bark. Bimba bark is also what the boys use to roof over the *mbanjo*. They cut a four or five-foot wide strip around the circumference of the tree, then with great force peel it off. Some men and boys lay similar bark strips over their beds as well as a kind of sleeping mattress; personally, I find bare poles more comfortable.

BaBenzélé huts tend to be a little more complicated in shape than the huts of the Ituri forest Efé, for example. The Efé make simple beehive huts. The BaBenzélé make the same shape huts, but if they will be spending more than a week in the same camp their huts often become more elaborate affairs. I love BaBenzélé architecture. It is a women's art of contours and roundness – asymmetrical, infinitely pleasing to the eye. Low igloo-like tunnels lead into the main chamber of some huts; in a few, the tunnel itself curves. Other huts consist of two or even three hemispheres connected by lower saddleback passages. Sometimes two hut complexes are joined together by a single new "hallway" chamber with a separate entrance for each household. Other huts have porches, a framework extension left partially or completely unleafed where the woman typically does her cooking. On the inside these huts are always surprisingly roomy, far more than one ever suspects when viewing them from the outside – an optical illusion of the subtle topology of their curves and surfaces.

boyobi

By nightfall on this first night in the forest the boys in the *mbanjo* are usually pounding away on a variety of drum substitutes. Soon the girls will sit near them and start to sing. It is only in these forest hunting camps that the music form *boyobi* comes into its own. From now on we will be in the domain of the *bobé,* the spirits associated with *boyobi*, and they will never be far from camp; they will always be reminding us of their existence, screaming out just before dawn or passing through camp in the dead of night, whistling weird melodies. Sometimes the lively chatter in camp in late afternoon, after the hunters have returned, will momentarily fall silent at the sharp report of a popping leaf from the surrounding forest, a sure indication of the *bobé's* presence. On a more folkloric level the *mokoondi* (spirits) thrive too: parents constantly invoke them to silence unreasonably crying children, like a kind of bogeyman who will come and take them away if he hears them crying. Occasionally parents go to quite elaborate lengths to persuade an obstinate child of the reality and imminence of a visit from a hungry or otherwise unfriendly spirit. Neighbors lend a hand in these subterfuges. Without even being asked, they tap the outside of the hut like something unpleasant is trying to force entrance, shout out that they've just seen the *mokoondi* and boy was it big, fake the sounds of a violent encounter in which they've just managed to drive the spirit away, expressing doubt that they will be able to do so again should the spirit return, as it undoubtedly will if the child keeps crying. Such a performance never fails to quiet the child.

Boyobi is performed now and then at village settlements like Yandoumbé, but a forest performance is a different experience. At Yandoumbé, the choir of women tends to be huge, as women from the various neighborhoods all come together to participate. During these ceremonies the magic is evident. Yandoumbé seems to be floating in its own private dimension; usually a mist isolates it from the rest of the world. The music itself is vast and wild and sometimes stunningly complex. In the forest *boyobi* is a more intimate affair; forest camps tend to be family-based and so the style of *boyobi* and the songs preferred may differ from one forest group to the next. In addition, unlike the village version, which usually is an isolated event and may be the only *boyobi* for weeks, *boyobi* in the forest may go on for weeks, rather the way in the village an *ejengi* ceremony may last months, with some days a lull in the music and other days scarcely a moment's rest. Unlike *ejengi*, however, the *bobé* are mainly nighttime visitors, and days are left free for hunting and gathering.

At night, in all but the smallest camps, *boyobi* rules. The *bobé* become a tangible presence. They come clothed in foliage or tree bark, or naked and white and faceless, wearing conical leaf hats, or in the ghostly glowing skeleton shapes of animals and bizarre creatures. They rip apart huts and charge at people unpredictably; it is dangerous to ignore them, or to wander away from the main group of people at a dance. Once I saw the *bobé* grab two young boys who, instead of tapping percussion, had fallen asleep on the ground. The traditional penalty for falling asleep during *boyobi* is death, and the women protested emotionally as the *bobé* carried the boys off into the forest. For some time the spirits' voices rose in shrieks and spooky discordant tunes, mingling with frightened whines from the boys. Later on during the ceremony, when the *bobé* were again dancing to the women's singing, they dropped a big bushy bundle onto the ground after a strenuous dance and scampered back into the forest. The bundle turned out to be the two boys, bound together with vines to a bunch of leafy branches and a log. They were shaken but none the worse for wear, and perhaps a little wiser.

One curious fact I have noticed is that little boys will play-act as *bobé* when they are holding a play ceremony with little girls. The little girls never imitate the *bobé*. This is at an age long before the boys know the connection between the men and the *bobé*, a connection similar to the one that exists between Clark Kent and Superman. And once I watched a five-year-old boy enact an entire *boyobi* ceremony by himself. He played drum on a plastic jerrycan while singing the women's chorus, then became the *bobé* and sang with a falsetto voice. He switched identities back and forth, and his solo performance (he wasn't even conscious of me watching him) lasted over an hour. The melodies he sang came from a *boyobi* held the previous night.

Just as the first night in a new forest camp is celebrated with *boyobi*, so the following dawn is greeted in all but the largest camps with the music form *makusé*. This delightful ceremony is performed to bring luck to a new camp literally, to draw food near. It begins at the crack of dawn, usually with rallying cries from the first man to wake up, and goes on until sunrise. Men and women emerge from their huts with hunting and gathering paraphernalia like baskets, crossbows, spears and axes, which they place leaning up around the base of a large tree. A small fire is lit around the tree as well, and as they sing the *makusé* songs everyone fans the tree trunk in unison with leafy branches. A kind of percussion is intermittently supplied by one or more men chopping at the tree with their axes, symbolizing honey-gathering. Once the sun is up the music is over and the day's activities begin. *Makusé* is a type of music one never hears in the village, and even in the forest I've never heard it performed more than once on any sojourn.

EJENGI – the most famous forest spirit of them all

hunting, gathering, singing

Most days camp empties out by eight, and often much sooner. No one but children, too big to carry but too small to keep up with the hunting party, and one or two elders remain behind. For these children forest life is of the utmost benefit. Many will have become sickly in the village, where the ubiquitous sand flea, the bane of Bayaka children, wreaks havoc on their feet, and where not enough to eat, too much sun and too many mosquitos have weakened them. For some, a move into the forest may mean a new lease on life. I went into the forest once with a family, the man of which had worked over a year for a student researching pangolins. During all that time the man had neglected to take his family to live in the forest even once. Now that the student had gone for good, he wanted to make up for lost time and was leading his family to a *payu* camp deep in the forest. His six-year-old daughter was a pathetic sight. She had so many infections from the sand fleas on her feet, she could hardly walk along the narrow path. She was skinny, a crybaby and terrified of the forest. I remember how tightly she clung to me when I carried her for a couple of miles. Three months later, still in the forest, she had fattened up and could run faster than many of the boys her age. Her personality had flowered – she had become a talkative little cutie. Those three months made a crucial difference to her prospects in life.

One of the favorite activities of the little children, both boys and girls, is to chop down saplings with a machete. This is not as wasteful an activity as one may suppose. Many of the saplings so cut do not die, but later sprout a new shoot; those that do succumb merely increase the survival odds for one of their

many competitors vying for the same niche. Most important, however, is that this chopping activity is how the children begin to develop that extraordinary accuracy with which adults wield their axes. In other play, too, the children are acquiring forest skills. They love to climb the small trees around camp, and they quickly pick up the trick of climbing a larger tree by shimmying up smaller neighboring trees, then switching over to the larger tree when they find a foothold. In a popular game, also played in roadside settlements, one boy sends half a round fruit rolling swiftly past a row of boys. They wield thin sharpened sticks, sometimes with a tiny metal blade forged from a piece of nail, which they hurl at the bouncing fruit as it speeds by. Quite often someone spears it.

Meanwhile the little girls might use similar fruits as dolls, carrying them like babies in straps of cloth along their side, under an arm. This is the Bayaka style for carrying children, as opposed to villager women, who carry their babies in a similar strip of cloth against their backs. The Bayaka method is far more intimate, for it allows eye contact and all kinds of verbal exchange between parent and child. The child has a view of the path ahead. Probably the method used by village women was adopted around the same time as agriculture. During long hours of stooping over in a field, a mother had to carry her baby on her back.

Teenagers usually take part in the net hunts, but the boys especially are apt to play hooky, preferring to go off on their own after birds with their small crossbows and un-poisoned arrows. They also lay little snares along the trails, made from vegetal fiber or homemade string, and often baited with tiny termite larvae like so much sprinkled rice. By such methods they catch francolins and guinea fowls, which they prepare and consume themselves in the *mbanjo*. The teenage girls are just as adept at finding themselves food, and come back from short expeditions with their own *koko* [edible leaf of a common forest vine (*Gnetum*)], various sorts of mushrooms, and the yam-like tuber *ékuli* (Dioscorea). Although they have no *mbanjo*, they usually erect a miniature beehive hut or two in which they play and cook their tidbits. They do not normally sleep in these play huts.

Camp life centers around the net hunt. While there may be individual men who do not participate (usually because they prefer to hunt with crossbow, a solo activity), the net hunt generally involves the entire community. The men are the principal net wielders, though frequently one or more women also command nets. These nets are made from rope that is fabricated out of the *nkusa* (*Manniophyton*) vine and measure about four feet high and fifty to eighty feet long. The men attach one end of the net to a sapling by means of a wooden hook, then move rapidly and silently through the bush stringing out the net behind them. Women and teenagers follow along and secure the net to roots and branches. Where one net ends the next begins, until finally they make a nearly closed circle. For some reason the circle is never fully closed.

The actual moments of the hunt are fascinating to hear. Sometimes there is a signal, a popping leaf, and then the silence which has been hanging in the air is broken by a series of rising whoops and yodeled yelps as the hunters, mostly the men, sweep through the enclosed forest with spears. The hunting cries grow more excited and purposeful once game is spotted (usually various duiker species). Once an animal is spotted they shout out its direction to one another. Women waiting at the perimeter of the circle listen carefully to these signals, and are always ready when an animal comes shooting out of the bush and into the net they are tending. Large duikers often break right through the nets and vanish into the forest, or leap over. Even the small blue duiker will only be delayed by the net for a few seconds and must be secured immediately. An animal belongs to the owner of the net in which it was caught, and is usually quartered and divided up on the spot. Complex rules dictate the way it is shared out. When all the animals of the area are deemed to have been caught or gotten away, the Bayaka gather up their nets and move on to the next promising location.

While moving through the forest the women take the opportunity to gather mushrooms, or nuts like *kana (Panda oleosa)* and *payu (Irvingia excelsa)*, or dig up wild yams. Sometimes wild fruits are found which provide a snack eaten on the spot. The men gather bundles of *nkusa*, to be converted step-by-step back at camp into rope. Everyone keeps an eye out for signs of honey in the treetops or tortoises on the forest floor.

A day's hunt is always a day of unique experiences, and so later afternoons when the hunting party returns to camp are always lively and filled with accounts of the day's adventures. Everyone has at least one story in which he or she is the star character. During this grand hour of socializing the men tend to congregate in the *mbanjo*, some of them stripping down the nkusa they brought back that day while they gossip. Others occupy themselves as they chat while fingering out the white kernels of the *payu* which will later be roasted and pounded and used in a spicy sauce. These tasks appear as effortless and automatic to them as knitting is among some experienced practitioners. Scarcely more attention-demanding are some of the tasks the women like to fill their "idle" time with, such as making their lovely reed baskets, so unique and aesthetically pleasing in shape, with their wide circular rims and small rectangular bottoms.

The little children who have endured their mothers' absences during the day and remained at camp now find their reward in the various snacks they are given to munch on: sweet edible roots like *mola* that are roasted in embers; pieces of meat, usually liver or heart, which they can grill up themselves and a leaf-wrapped bundle of *kuma*, a honey made by a species of small stingless bee.

It is this hour as afternoon changes to evening that the children, in high spirits, play their musical games. These games have always fascinated me. Each game has its own accompanying musical round, and these pairings of song and game seem to be passed from one generation of children to the next with little change. Who knows but some of them might be very old. I find them among the most difficult musical events to record. Often the children's singing is scarcely more than fragmentary, as they interrupt themselves with outbursts of hilarity, arguments, mischievous side-pranks. And on some occasions when I've produced my microphones to record a promising session the adults have ruined everything by sternly admonishing the children, telling them not to make any noise while they sang. The children (who were doing quite well on their own, thank you) ceased playing the games altogether and, with no spontaneity, merely stood in one place singing the songs. Nevertheless, over the years I've managed to make a few nice recordings. Much less frequently one hears these games in roadside settlements; they are more characteristic of forest life.

A switch in the opposite direction concerns the teenagers' dance *elanda*. One of the most popular dances at Yandoumbé, *elanda* is totally forgotten in the forest. Perhaps its absence supports the claims of many Bayaka that *elanda* is a dance they acquired many ages ago from Bayaka in the savanna to the north.

Day after day the net hunters go out. At first they scarcely leave the vicinity of camp, and the hunts take place within earshot. Later the hunts move farther afield. Meanwhile, all sorts of individual activities complement the main occupation of hunting. Most camps have at least one crossbow expert, and this kind of hunting demands individual effort: stealth, marksmanship and the strength of the poison the hunter has brewed up and coated onto the arrow tips are the determining factors, as is the make of the crossbow. Some skilled crossbow hunters can't make decent crossbows and commission their weapons from others who can. Even on days when the net hunt fails, a crossbow hunter may yet return with something for the pot – monkey or duiker, usually. Families go off to collect *booey* (honey), the kind the honeybees make, usually found near the tops of the very tallest trees. Teenage buddies may go off to chop down one of the smaller (though still considerably large) trees that contain the liquid honey *kuma*. These sweet additions for the camp diet are welcomed and craved by men, women and children alike.

Eventually there will come a consensus to move camp. Perhaps the hunters feel they have emptied the area of game; if no one has had any luck finding *booey*, this may be sufficient reason to change locations; sometimes it's the knowledge of better forest ahead that draws the Bayaka on, or a discovery of lots of *payu*, or an abundant supply of *ékuli*, among the main sources of carbohydrates in the forest. If the Bayaka linger too long in one place, some of the same problems that plague them in the village settlement will begin to arise here: sand fleas, in the form of eggs in the feet of the children, may have been carried out to camp and after a couple of weeks they start to hatch. Infestation will intensify rapidly if the camp is not abandoned. Only after they have moved camp several times and remained in the forest two months do the Bayaka rid themselves completely of these nasty parasites. Problems of sanitation never become dilemmas in the forest as long as the Bayaka keep moving.

And so one morning, munching on a few snacks, everyone assembles their gear and packs it away. The women clear the huts of their protective layers of branches and then disassemble them *ngungu* leaf by

ngungu leaf. Good *ngungu* leaves may be hard to come by at the next campsite and are never left behind. They are always packed and taken along. They are used and reused until they start to crumble.

The women's carrying baskets have an astonishing capacity. In addition to kitchen gear like pots and bowls and leftover food items (usually packed in a way that affords easy access during the march) they hold whatever clothes the family owns, hunting nets, reed mats rolled and folded, and on top of everything else and towering well above the women carrying them, the bundles of *ngungu* leaves tied and lashed with vines to the basketload below. Teenage girls normally carry similar but smaller baskets, while the teenage boys, in addition to their modest spears, seem to specialize in single heavy items, like the big wooden *kingil* (mortars) in which the women pound various food items.

The men usually carry a spear over the left shoulder, holding it by the shaft just behind the blade, which points forward. Next to the spear an axe rests balanced over the shoulder, blade at the back and handle down the front. In their right hand they wield a machete. Round one side of the neck runs the strap for their *mata*, a small cylindrical case with a cover made from stiff duiker hide. In this container they keep various important items: their fire kit (small chunks of a flammable tree resin called *vaka*, and nowadays also matches); their medical kit (a razor, packets of medicinal barks, roots and leaves and a small black hollow blue duiker's horn, used as a suction device over the skin when applying traditional medicines); their smoking kit (a cigarette or plug of tobacco, a pinch of cannabis, perhaps a homemade cigarette holder); and various odds and ends. Crossbow hunters in addition have their crossbows and their large duiker-hide satchels in which they carry poisoned arrows (in their own bamboo cylinder), arrows not yet poisoned, and other paraphernalia associated with crossbow hunting. The men prefer to go forward in this relatively unburdened state well in advance of the rest of the group, in the hopes of encountering game like duikers or bushpigs. Frequently, however, they must take their turn carrying one or another of their children.

The women have a great fear of running into gorillas while on the march. As a typical educated Westerner, I'm familiar with the work of Schaller, Fossey and others and "know" that gorillas will not harm me if I sit still with my eyes to the ground. I've told this to the Bayaka countless times. Their reply has always been the same: "Hey! If that works for you, then go with it. But gorillas don't like Bayaka! As soon as they see us they go nuts." I've pointed out that maybe the gorillas have good cause to get excitable, seeing all those spears being flourished and waved about. One conclusion I've reached: encountering a gorilla when in the company of the Bayaka is a frightening and dangerous experience. Usually to everyone's relief (mine especially) the gorillas scream in terror and flee immediately. But sometimes a courageous male will make a stand and challenge our approach with a powerful roar. Then the Bayaka men roar back. For one suspenseful moment there is a kind of balance of terror as Bayaka match lung power against the gorilla. In every incident I've witnessed the gorilla has been intimidated and retreated, but I've heard of instances in which the gorilla has become so riled up that it charged. After one such instance at which I wasn't present, the hunting party returned bearing one of their own: he'd been bitten in the buttocks as he fled the gorilla. The wound healed. Students researching gorillas have told me how one or another of their untrained Bayaka guides has reacted to a gorilla charge by charging back at the gorilla!

The Bayaka may remain out in the forest anywhere from a week to nine or ten months. Sometimes they stay in one general vicinity, and sometimes they move deeper and deeper into the forest and then gradually make their way back again. When a group is not too far from the village, men and women make trips to the village to replenish supplies. First and foremost these include manioc and salt. Tobacco is high on the list of men's priorities, although they make due for long periods without.

Manioc in particular poses a problem. A relatively recent addition to the Bayaka diet (better known as cassava, manioc comes from Brazil and was only introduced into Africa at the beginning of the 16th century), manioc has become their staple source of carbohydrates. When they live by the road the Bayaka eat manioc with every meal. When they depart for the forest, they carry as much manioc as they can lay their hands on. Formerly this manioc would have been obtained through barter or labor from the villagers, but nowadays the Bayaka have their own fields and the manioc they take with them into the forest is manioc they have grown themselves.

Once in the forest the Bayaka supplement their carbohydrate intake with various wild "yams." These make an excellent and tasty substitute but their abundance and availability is irregular. Large tracts of the forest seem to be without edible tubers, and they cannot be depended on for a sustained daily supply. As long as the Bayaka remain within fifteen miles of the village, they will make occasional trips to get more manioc. As they move farther out such supply runs become less practical and finally stop altogether. Although the Bayaka love manioc, and are practically addicted to its high concentration of carbohydrates (over ninety percent), small groups especially are quite adept at going without it, once they are truly into their forest mode (meaning they would rather remain in the forest even if there's no smoke and no manioc). Small camps can sustain themselves with the occasional wild yam find. These wild yams are not actually yams but various kinds of tuber, a couple of which taste remarkably like ordinary potatoes. Since time immemorial the Bayaka have in fact practiced a rudimentary kind of agriculture with some of these edible tubers, which can grow from cuttings taken from their vines, by planting "gardens" of these cuttings deep in the forest.

When in season, the large flat seeds of the bimba tree fall in super abundance. Using a thorny stick, the Bayaka grate the tough flesh of these seeds into a powder, and this powder can be mixed with boiling water to make a kind of sticky paste that can serve as a manioc substitute. When none of these substitutes is available, the Bayaka simply do without. Once I lived in a camp where we ate nothing but bushpig and honeycomb for two weeks, before deciding to move on somewhere else where wild yams grew plentifully.

Eventually the time comes when the forest party decides to return to the village. Sometimes rain becomes so frequent that net hunting is no longer a viable means of support. Sometimes the decision to return is prompted by the desire or need to work on their manioc plantations. Once I was with a group that was chased away by the park patrol who told us (mistakenly, as it turned out) that we were in the national park. Once in a while a death is what triggers a return to the road.

For me there is always a sense of regret upon leaving the forest. The Bayaka men, I know, experience the return to the village in a different way. Their forest selves express regret at the departure, but as soon as their feet touch the road they switch over to their village personalities and are excited to be back. Many of them will be heading into town within an hour of their touchdown at Yandoumbé, to see what they can score to smoke or drink. I too will switch into my village mode, but the transition comes less easily to me, and it will take days. Right now, I blink at the open sky as we step out of the forest, from the comforting twilight into bright afternoon sunshine. I will miss the intimacy of our little group, our nights of *boyobi* and *gano*. Our remoteness and isolation in the forest had turned us into a self-contained social group. We had relied only upon each other for all our needs. I remember the deep contentment and feeling of coming home I always experienced when I arrived back at camp after a day's wandering in the woods. Now, reaching Yandoumbé, there is an explosion of my world horizon. Everyone, and soon me too, is turned outward. In the forest our human community was enclosed on all sides by wild nature and we were the only people on earth, but here at Yandoumbé the human community stretches right across the entire planet. We have rejoined the mainstream of humanity, and the shock of it is always a little frightening.

Mondumu (drums)

A medium to large hollowed-out log with the skin of a duiker (*mbom* is the species preferred because of its tough hide) stretched over the top and secured by large wooden pegs. At Yandoumbé many men (and women) admitted to me that the drum was copied from a villager design, and went on to say that unlike many villager things, drums are good. Since then the BaBenzélé have become such accomplished drummers that their indigenous neighbors, whose lives traditionally revolve around fishing on the Sangha river, always require a BaBenzélé drum and drummer for their own funeral rites. Yandoumbé has made, used and discarded many wooden drums, but its pride and joy has always been a big steel cylinder with a deep and powerful tone. This drum has been around since my earliest days with the Bayaka, and its tone is so famous and desirable that on many occasions the local town authorities confiscate it to use in official functions like parades and dances to greet important visitors. Sometimes Yandoumbé doesn't get its drum back for a week. In former times one type of drum used was made from a strip of bark bent into a cylinder. For a skin, white latex sap from certain liana species was spread over one's belly and chest, then after it had dried into a thin rubber sheet it was peeled off and stretched over both ends of the bark cylinder several times. When struck the proper way these drums give off a deep drawn-out vibrating sound, like a revving engine. In forest camps children still make small toy ones to play with.

Geedal (bow harp)

A sound box covered on top with (these days) a thin sheet of metal; at one end a hole into which is inserted a wood bow from a tree; six tuning pegs along this bow adjust the tones of the nylon strings whose other ends are attached in a straight row along the middle of the sound box. Bow harps exist among many if not most peoples in central Africa, and among many beyond. The Bayaka bow harp usually has less strings than the others. Among the Efé it typically has five strings only. Among the BaBenzélé at Yandoumbé the instrument has six strings. Once I watched Mamadu make a new *geedal*. Balonyona borrowed it one day shortly after it was finished, but kept running into difficulties as he played. Finally he stopped to count the strings (to himself in French): "Un, deux, trois, quatre, cinq, six, SEPT!" The geedal had an unprecedented seven strings. That was the reason Balonyona had been thrown off in his playing. I noticed that no one, not even Mamadu, used this seventh string. When it broke it wasn't replaced. The *geedal* is a very popular instrument, and most boys teach themselves to play a tune or two on it. By the Bayaka's own admission, it is an instrument whose form originally came from a villager instrument. But the Bayaka have made it their own, and the sparkling strains of a *geedal* in the early evening as food is being cooked and social visits are at their peak is one of the defining experiences of life in a BaBenzélé settlement.

Mondumé (harp-zither)

A long (nearly four feet) stick with a tall perpendicular bridge at its center; three nylon strings go from one end of the pole through a slot in the bridge to the other end of the pole; the string halves on either side of the bridge are different lengths, so the *mondumé* has six notes. All the BaBenzélé I talked to agree that it is an original Bayaka instrument. I have never seen anything like it among any other people. Because it has no sound box, the *mondumé* has a soft, barely audible tone, so usually it is pressed across a big open pot while being played. The pot not only amplifies the sound of the *mondumé* but itself often reverberates, modulating the notes in weird and interesting ways. Sometimes certain notes cause a sympathetic vibration in the pot, which rattles and surrounds the notes with fuzz noise, an effect the BaBenzélé like. My favorite player is Mabuti, who has a poet's touch with every note he plays; sometimes his playing reaches a Zen-like state of simplicity and purity that can hold me in a spell. Another formidable player is Mobila, who has a vigorous style and can play for hours without pause, his performance one of immense improvisation in which melody flows into melody. Today the *mondumé* is alive and well at Yandoumbé and there are a number of talented players. However, none are younger than middle age and perhaps eventually the *mondumé* may become more rare.

Mbyo (notched flute)

A hollow vegetal tube, one end plugged with black resin, the playing end with a V-shaped notch cut into the rim; four equally-spaced stops. The *mbyo* is an end-blown flute. According to the BaBenzélé it is one of their original instruments. As far as I know no one else in the Dzanga-Sangha region has such an instrument, although end-blown flutes are one of the most widespread and ancient of all instruments, occurring in many cultures worldwide and even depicted in prehistoric rock art. The *mbyo* is usually a solo instrument. It is played alone, almost always at night. Yandoumbé has three accomplished *mbyo* players: Contreboeuf, his younger brother Mobila (the same Mobila who also plays the *mondumé*), and Gongé, who at about thirty-five years old is the youngest player. Contreboeuf is the true *mbyo* genius, having completely mastered the "yodel technique" of playing, wherein a melody contains rapid leaps between octaves that are like abbreviated trills. Rendered swiftly and flawlessly, such a technique creates the impression of two flutes playing at the same time, as the notes in the lower register take on a "life" and melody of their own, completely separate from the sequence of notes in the upper register, which spell out a different melody. It is a kind of one-voiced polyphony. Thanks largely to Contreboeuf, the voice of the *mbyo* is familiar to young and old alike at Yandoumbé. Elderly and thin, with a long neck and large eyes, Contreboeuf is like some rare nocturnal bird as he rises typically at three in the morning and, wandering slowly around Yandoumbé, plays until five. Melodies pour forth into the night, punctuated by his famous trademark trill.

Other Instruments

Rattles come in many forms at Yandoumbé: from comparatively elaborate models made from the same material used for the carrying baskets and filled with seeds, to simple seed pods either singly or in bunches, to tin cans scrunched up with pebbles trapped inside, to little plastic ones made in China. Rattles are most commonly used in lullabies, but are also an important element in the women's music *limboku*. Sometimes the rattle is used in *ejengi, boyobi, gano,* etc.

In appearance the *mbindi* (earth bow) is one of the most basic of all instruments: a piece of rope (usually made from fibers of the *nkusa* vine) is tied to the top of a sapling, and this sapling is bent over into a bow shape as the other end of the rope is pegged firmly into the ground. The rope is then plucked, and the tone raised or lowered by lightly pushing or pulling the sapling to vary the tension. The sound is normally a deep bass, and many of the typical riffs sound jazz-like. The *mbindi* is played for amusement, primarily in forest camps, always constructed on the spot in a minute or two.

An interesting variation of the *mbindi* is the hut bow, in which the rope is attached to one of the flexible poles in the ceiling of a traditional beehive hut instead of to a sapling. The tone is varied by pushing or pulling on the hut pole. The hut bow is played by women and is not commonly seen (in all my years I've only seen it twice). I'm told it also exists among the Efé in the Ituri forest.

Toy kazoos are made by children from scraps of cellophane. Men use a kazoo in their secret *so* ceremony, where it is one of two or three different spirit voices.

On occasion I have seen the men play a short transversely-blown bamboo trumpet. This was used in the men's *so* and also sometimes in *makusé*. I have also heard the men imitate the sound of this instrument when returning from successful spear hunts.

The men have told me intriguing stories about the ceremonies that used to surround a successful elephant hunt. Part of these involved the use of a bull roar, or flying rhomb. This was played by the men on their return to camp. Women had to hide in their huts during the sound of this deep spirit voice which announced the death of the elephant. The flying rhomb is an instrument that has been found among many hunter-gatherer societies around the world, including tribes like the Bororo of the Mato Grosso in Brazil, the aboriginal Australians and Khoisan groups like the Kung. Among all of these peoples the sound of the bull-roar is associated with spirits. So far no example has ever been documented among any of the Bayaka in central Africa, and I fear that none will. Like spearhunting for elephant, use of the flying rhomb is a tradition that has already vanished.

I have found no tradition of the *sanza* ("thumb piano") among the BaBenzélé, although they know the instrument from Baya immigrants to the nearby town from the northern savanna, where there is a rich *sanza* tradition. For some reason the BaBenzélé show no interest in learning to play it themselves. However, once when the government obliged myself and a team of BaBenzélé from Yandoumbé to participate in a national harvest and folklore festival being held at Bossongoa in the north, we met an old Baya *sanza* player who used to visit us and play his songs. He was a big hit with the Bayaka, and when we returned to Yandoumbé Balonyona remembered one of the old man's *sanza* songs well enough to transcribe it for *geedal*. It is now part of the standard bow-harp repertoire.

Some crossbow hunters make a three-holed whistle from a large oval seed. It plays two high notes which sound like the cry of a monkey-hunting eagle. The hunters use the whistle to flush out any monkeys in the canopy.

For the rest, the BaBenzélé use many unaltered natural objects to produce sounds which they incorporate into their music, such as the *koondi* water drum. Other objects are associated with *mokoondi*. One of the spirits' characteristic sounds is the popping leaf: a loose fist is made with a leaf on top, then the leaf is popped by slapping it over the hollow of the fist. The *mokoondi* frequently drum the ground by slapping it very hard with open palms. Earth percussion is also occasionally used to accompany the *geedal* and earth bow. The *mokoondi* also use sticks to thwack huts loudly during and in-between songs, and are also very fond of whistling.

visual art

Among the BaBenzélé visual art is minimal and exclusively decorative. Possibly once, as the Efé still do today, the BaBenzélé made bark cloth, and the women painted abstract designs on this cloth. But the bark cloth tradition has died out along the Sangha River, and now the most obvious example of visual art left is the *matelé* or tattoos. These are blue designs done mostly on the face and forehead, and also (for women) on the arms, stomach and legs. These tattoos are like fragments of bark cloth paintings. No two are alike. They are not done on any regular schedule, as far as I know. The cuts are made with a razor and then a black paste made from a forest plant *(Rothmania)* is smeared into the wounds.

A more striking visual art can be seen in the glowing designs of the *bobé*. At night the forest floor is speckled with a bioluminescent mold that grows on flecks of decaying vegetation, but I personally have never seen anything like the solid bars of bioluminescence that decorate the *bobé*. And the manner of their attachment to the body remains mysterious. Sometimes a piece falls off, but considering the wild movements of the *bobé*, these big glowing bars are secured in place remarkably well. The occasional piece that does fall is never left lying there for long. Its *bobé* owner will always whisk it away with him into the forest. They never forget a piece.

my lifestyle changes

I suppose one of the main stumbling blocks in people's minds when they contemplate my permanent change of address is the thought of all that I had to "give up" to make the move to the rain forest. What they don't understand is that from my point of view I gave up very little. For instance, a house has never seemed to me to be anything more than a fancy and ingenious way of boxing up a little parcel of space. The idea of putting myself in debt for the next quarter century so that I can spend most of my life in this parcel of space and end up its proud owner before I die has never appealed to me as one of life's rational options. Naturally I don't begrudge such an option to anyone else, and I'm well aware that in some important sense our entire civilization depends on this option being pursued by the majority of people.

Likewise I have never felt the temptation to purchase an automobile. In fact, I believe automobiles are a curse on this planet, and that the internal combustion engine in particular is one of the worst and most wasteful inventions in history. I hate the poisoning of the air they cause, and the destruction that roads bring, especially to the rain forest. I abhor the noise of the internal combustion engine, which is becoming increasingly difficult to escape.

As for television, I grew up glued to it. Theme songs from many a forgotten series and commercial still pop up to irk me now and then, especially during malaria fevers. I have never missed it in the least. I can say the same for radio and in particular the news. I prefer going long periods without "the news." Think of it: the Berlin Wall had been down a month before I heard about it, a rare and wonderful surprise.

The only major item of luxury I imagine owning now and then is a superb sound system, mostly in order to play my recordings of their music back to the Bayaka. They simply love to listen to their own music, and I love to listen to it with them.

What about food? Surely I must miss some of the foods I grew up with?

I do. *Koko (Gnetum buchholzianum)* is the edible leaf of a creeper and grows in super abundance in many parts of the forest, but it is the only leafy green from the forest that the Bayaka regularly eat. So there are days when I would like to eat a great big salad, with three kinds of lettuce, two kinds of endive, tomatoes, cucumbers and fresh basil. Why don't I grow a garden? I would, but I'm always moving into the forest and am never around long enough to raise any plants.

The other serious craving that occasionally grips me is for sugar. It always seizes me in the forest, when bad luck has resulted in a scarcity of food, and we are all hungry. Then I can't help but start to imagine all the different sweet foods available for a fiver in Manhattan, like chocolate ice cream, or hot buckwheat pancakes smothered in genuine maple syrup, or twelve-ounce brownies home-baked on the premises, or

macadamia nut cookies as big as dinner plates, or cheesecake so rich it takes a mouthful a whole minute to reach your stomach after you swallow. But then, as so often happens when there's nothing else to eat, someone returns to camp in the evening with a pot of honeycomb that took him all day to collect. Most of the contents he reserves for his family, but there are several leaf bundles (honeycomb wrapped up in layers of *ngungu* leaves and tightly knotted close with vine) which are pre-wrapped gifts for various people. I receive mine with hungry excitement, secretly disappointed only by its modest size, which means there won't be any left over to eat in the middle of the night; in the beginning my capacity to gorge myself on honeycomb could accommodate no more than a heaping tablespoon's worth, but these days I can and do wolf down a pound of the stuff in thirty seconds flat.

The sun's down, the bees gone, so I untie my bundle and peel back the leaves to reveal: three slabs of comb dripping in honey. Honeycombs come in all sorts of stages: the kind that's filled not so much with honey as with soft white larvae that are juicy rather than sweet; the very old molasses-brown brittle comb with its malty flavor; the new young comb, buttery white and more delicate than a wafer, that in the mouth dissolves into pure liquid honey, a favorite of many Bayaka; there's the slightly older wax comb laden with golden "supermarket" honey. And then there's my favorite kind, its chambers packed with bright orange pollen, its wax extensively mixed with propolis; when I bite off a piece it bursts with a swirl of perfumey flavors and tastes like a cake made of candied flowers imported from paradise. And instead of that chewing-gum never-ready-to-swallow feeling that comes from chewing the waxier combs, this one eventually crumbles in the mouth like fudge.

Every time I eat it I reach the same conclusion: wild honeycomb is one of the most blissful taste sensations on planet Earth, and one mouthful is enough to banish for a month all my atavistic cravings for the complete works of Häagen-Dazs and Pepperidge Farm combined.

Last but not least, nothing really beats a sweet juicy peach. The rain forest may be loaded with all kinds of edible fruits like big three-lobed berries with a refreshing tangy taste reminiscent of sour cherry; or small white-fleshed fruits that taste like "I-can't-believe-they're-not-lichis"; or the ever-popular liana fruits known collectively as *mavundu (Landolphia)* that look like lumpy thick-skinned grapefruits and oranges, but which when split open with a blow of the fist reveal a globular mass of fleshy lobes either white, pink or bright red that are swallowed pit and all, lobe by lobe, and that all taste like honeydew; or the giant irregularly oblong green fruit called *mbé (Anonidium mannii)* that falls with a far-carrying head-crushing thud and whose orange flesh with its sweet-potatoey flavor is so rich in protein that in a real fix its ripe pasty flesh eaten salted and spiced with chilies makes a delicious substitute meal. In my opinion none of these can match a peach, and I always wanted one day to be able to turn my Bayaka friends on to the delights of the peach. In June 1991 I got my chance, when I met them in Paris.

Sixteen BaBenzélé from Yandoumbé, eleven men and five women, were invited by the former first lady of

France to perform in the fourth annual African Music Festival in Paris. At the time I was in New York, so the Festival organizers flew me to Paris to meet my friends when they arrived after their first plane ride. We were given a large studio room at the Parc de la Villette to camp in, where we cooked our meals on hotplates and slept on lightweight aluminum cots dormitory style. A young Frenchman named Nabil was assigned to cater to the Bayaka's every food whim (they brought their own manioc, but nothing else except for a sack of finely chopped *koko* that had spoiled on route). I had insisted on bottled water, and Nabil delivered a carload, backing up his vehicle to a special studio door so that he could offload the three hundred bottles directly into our studio. The Bayaka were impressed. Then Nabil drove off again to go purchase the four crates of honey the Bayaka insisted was absolutely necessary for their well-being. Nabil had been given an unlimited budget by the festival committee to carry out his function. He loved getting the Bayaka anything they asked for. For their part the Bayaka thought he was just someone who had befriended them, and they were truly amazed by his generosity. Nabil brought us a hundred pounds of bananas, two crates of oranges, ten pineapples, five pounds of cherries, five pounds of strawberries, and, at my personal request a crate of peaches. The Bayaka took full advantage of a cornucopia that would become legendary by the time they returned to Yandoumbé and about which stories are still told today. They ate and ate, steering clear only of those foods unfamiliar to them, including, despite my recommendation, the peaches. Those men bold enough even to taste one (the women refused) made faces and never touched one again. The only unknown fruit for which they developed a taste was cherries. I remember Balonyona coming over to me angrily after he ate his first cherry. "These are really delicious!" he declared, holding one up in front of my face. "Why didn't you tell us about them! They've been sitting around here for days getting rotten!"

conservation

Tropical rain forests throughout the world are under threat, and the forests of Central Africa are no exception. For more than two decades the forests have been selectively logged, so that what remains now in the Dzanga-Sangha region is a patchwork of primary forest and secondary forest in various stages of recovery or current destruction. Selective logging is not necessarily as devastating as clear-cutting, and if left alone for a long time such "harvested" forests may regain a healthy equilibrium. Some animals like the lowland gorilla actually seem to prefer secondary forests because of the more abundant herbaceous growth. Nevertheless, over time even a rotating form of selective logging will degrade the forest beyond healthy recovery.

Logging has more insidious effects too. The roads into the forest which logging companies construct to carry out their operations become highways into previously inaccessible forest, and these are taken full advantage of by illegal hunters who shoot animals with guns or trap them with wire snares for the meat trade. Logging also attracts new immigrants to the region, who come in search of employment, settle down, and all too often assault the forest with more slash and burn agriculture.

The Sangha forest region of the Central African Republic and down river in northern Congo and southwestern Cameroon has seen several boom-bust cycles (rubber, ivory, coffee, timber). Today logging continues in Cameroon, and has recently been resumed in the Central African Republic. In Congo there are ambitious plans to expand existing logging operations.

In the Central African Republic two blocks of forest have been set aside as national parks (Dzanga and Ndoki) where no economic activities of any kind are permitted. The forest between these two parks is a special reserve (Dzanga-Sangha) where limited and (in theory) renewable forms of exploitation are allowed. These include traditional hunting and gathering by the Bayaka, but unfortunately also hunting by licensed guns and logging. During its current boom, Bayanga, the major population center within the Dzanga-Sangha Reserve, has seen an influx of guns, and the use of wire snares has become extensive. The conservation infrastructure has been hard-pressed to counter the intensified poaching. The pressures of a boomtown economy are simply too powerful.

Across the border in the Congo the Nouabalé-Ndoki park has recently been passed into law. Like the two parks in Central African Republic, no economic activities of any kind are permitted in this park, including subsistence hunting and gathering by Bayaka. From the wildlife conservation viewpoint this park area is fortunate, for it has no permanent inhabitants, although the northern half of it has always been used by the BaBenzélé, for whom no allowance has currently been made.

Negotiations are underway to establish a park-reserve system in Cameroon, contiguous with Dzanga-Sangha. The main sponsors of this tri-national conservation effort are the World Wildlife Fund and the Wildlife Conservation Society, with input from the World Bank and other organizations.

So far the Bayaka have been at best peripheral to these conservation schemes. The Bayaka within the Dzanga-Sangha Reserve have seen a drastic reduction in the area of forest to which they have legal access. They have been hemmed in on three sides by national parks. The last small patch of primary rain forest open to them is under constant threat of logging. No part of the forest has been set aside for their exclusive use, even though they are the only people in the region who need the forest. What little forest remains to them is heavily poached and open to logging.

Traditionally the Bayaka have never posed a threat to the rain forest. They have hunted and gathered in these forests for a millennium at least, and still the densities of wildlife like lowland gorillas and forest elephants remain among the highest in Africa. Personally, I deplore the sheer extent of the forest which has been forbidden to the Bayaka. This forest is their heritage first and foremost, and only secondarily is it "our" (humanity's) heritage. The Bayaka have not abused their heritage in any significant way, and we who have abused ours have no moral right to take it away from them. While it is true that, given the modern means to do so (such as guns or plenty of wire snares), the Bayaka are just as capable of overexploiting the forest as the villagers in Bayanga, I believe that any conservation program must accept an obligation to seek ways in which the Bayaka eventually may be allowed access to protected areas of the forest in order to pursue their traditional hunting and gathering while at the same time not allowing other activities, especially logging. The Bayaka know the forest intimately; it is still necessary for their physical and spiritual well-being, and as yet there is no viable alternative to replace the forest in their lives.

Change is coming to the Bayaka as it has to everyone else. Much of this change is in the form of pressures to assimilate into the national societies of the countries in which they have their permanent settlements. Many of these changes are pressed upon them through an increasingly mercantile world. And some of these changes reflect the Bayaka's own choices. Increasingly, they want education in their own schools, and I foresee a time when many, given a genuine and viable alternative, will choose to turn their backs on their forest traditions. However, a core group of forest specialists will always remain, given the forest in which to carry out their traditions, and I believe they should not only be allowed to continue, but be actively encouraged and supported in this way of life. It is simply too priceless to allow to vanish.

1 WOMEN GATHERING MUSHROOMS

Early one morning seven women went a short way from a recently established forest camp to gather some mushrooms they had discovered the evening before. New forest camps often have a special feel of luxury, as all sorts of foods can be found in their immediate vicinity, and for the several days the task of food gathering is practically a romp. Mushroom gathering lends itself especially well to lyrical accompaniment, for it is not in the least bit strenuous and often (as here) takes place in beautiful and spacious primary forest. On this occasion from 1993 the women sang melodies from a *boyobi* ceremony they had sung the night before. I recorded from a short distance away. Afterward we all returned to camp and had a delicious mushroom breakfast. The entire expedition had taken little more than an hour.

The acoustics of the primary rain forest bestow on the human voice a special richness of tone. Yodels–calls or cries in which there is a transition between chest and throat voice–are the most natural and effective way to use the voice in this environment, because as the voice resonates through the trees both high and low notes hang in the air at the same time. A single voice thus creates a chord. For some reason yodels carry farther in the forest that ordinary shouts or screams, a fact I was able to verify once when I got momentarily lost. I howled and shrieked to no avail, and only when I began to yodel did others hear me. Everyone who meets the Bayaka is impressed by the power of their voices. From an early age, just about every individual in a Bayaka community goes through an informal but nonetheless rigorous voice training. Their vocal chords are exercised on a daily basis during expeditions into the forest and on hunts. The forest seems to invite them to cry out and hear the reverberation of their voices fade away. The women and girls are especially vocal in the forest, and by the time they are teenagers they develop voices of astonishing power and purity. These voices rival and surpass the voice of any opera singer, for that quality of tension one can detect in so many operatic voices is wholly absent from the Bayaka's. Having developed such extraordinary voices, it only seems natural that the Bayaka would have a musical tradition based upon the human voice.

2 WALKING SONG

Unlike the *geedal* the *mondumé* is an original Bayaka instrument. Technically it is a kind of harp zither. It is generally played with the forefingers of both hands, though once I listened to a player who also used his right thumb. As it does not have its own resonating chamber, the *mondumé* is usually placed over a pot to amplify its sound. It has a lighter, more delicate tone than the *geedal* and is splendidly suited for the acoustics of the forest. Most forest camps have at least one *mondumé* while one rarely encounters the instrument in village camps, where the *geedal* reigns supreme. Adamo, who plays in this recording from 1994, is peculiar in that he utilizes a tiny coffee can instead of a cooking pot as a resonating chamber. He can therefore play the *mondumé* while walking, which he often does. Here he performs his favorite "walking song."

3 BOYOBI AT SPEAR-HUNTING CAMP (PART ONE)

Boyobi, the ceremony performed before net and spear hunts to ensure success and protect the hunters from harm, represents the supreme musical artistry of the Bayaka. In no other form do so many elements of their musical genius appear together to find such full expression. Men, women and even children sing, creating at times a polyphony of stunning beauty and complexity; their percussion is often elaborate and may involve three drums as well as numerous accessories like pots, logs and sticks; and the weird and discordant cries of the *bobé*, the name for the spirits who dance in *boyobi,* add yet another dimension to the sound.

Although sometimes performed in village settlements, *boyobi* is above all a music of forest camps, where there is a hunt almost every day. In fact sometimes life in the forest becomes one long ceremony, interspersed with pauses for hunting, eating and sleeping. The song presented here comes from one such week-long *boyobi*, and took place at dawn, picking up where the ceremony left off only three or four hours before. The *bobé* appeared to dance, dressed in leaves and branches. As real drums had not yet been made at this camp, the drumming was expertly done on plastic jerrycans. Between twelve and fifteen women sang, as well as several girls and up to six men. Teenage boys as usual were the percussionists.

Boyobi represents several problems for the recordist. Often it takes place in absolute darkness and not even the glow from a drawn-on cigarette is tolerated. There is no secure place to set up microphones, for the *bobé* make wild unpredictable movements and nowhere is safe from their charges. Frequently the recordist must move rapidly to avoid getting knocked over by the *bobé*. The chorus of women is often split up in separate family groups sitting in various directions, making them difficult to record all at once. In addition, the voices of the *bobé* crying or singing out from the forest are often worth recording.

4 WEDDING SONG

Marriage is generally a casual affair among the Bayaka, in that there is no regular ceremony to celebrate it. Some marriages begin clandestinely as teenage affairs known only to the couple's intimate peers. The approved procedure, however, is for the young man to inform the girl's parents of his interest. With their approval he begins his courtship with gifts of meat, honey and even labor. If the girl accepts her suitor, her parents give the final go-ahead and the couple begin sleeping together, and soon move into their own separate home in the neighborhood of her parents. Occasionally on the night before they could sleep together, the women including the bride perform *limboku,* wandering slowly through the camp or roadside settlement singing and dancing, their movements highly charged with sexual innuendo. They surround a central figure, covering her from all eyes while she conjures up the female spirit named *limboku,* heard as a deep hooting voice. *Limboku,* is strictly off limits to boys and men, who are more or less confined to their houses during a performance. The track included here comes from a recording I made at Amapolo in 1989. The women allowed me to record them for about an hour of their all-night performance. Around thirty women participated.'

5 BENEDICTION ON A SETTLEMENT

Yeyi (which means yodel) is another form of women's music in which men do not normally take part, although since no *mokoondi* is evoked, the men's exclusion is not nearly so strictly enforced as in the case of *limboku. Yeyi* is performed to bring benediction on a camp or settlement. Typically it begins in the small hours of the morning with the yodels of a single woman, who earlier has drunk "medicine" to aid her in the ceremony. Soon her yodels are answered by others. The women come together, and as in *limboku* they wander through the settlement and nearby forest singing the special *yeyi* songs. During the course of the ceremony more and more women join in. This recording I made at Yondumbé in 1991. The singing began during the final moments of a thunderstorm. I recorded through the window of my house. In the song presented here the women (five or six) are on the move in my direction. They continued singing well into the dawn, by which time about a dozen women were involved, the ceremony ending as usual as the women wandered a final time through the village throwing leaves on the roof of each house. The main singer was a woman named Eloka.

6 BOYOBI (PART TWO)

It is night, and the boyobi started already days before is resumed yet again. In this track the whistles and high falsetto voices of the *bobé* can clearly be heard as *bobé* arrived in a bewildering array of green phosphorescent body designs. Animals, beings, headless creatures, even military-like figures with glowing shoulder pads appeared and vanished in the course of the night, dancing and charging about with reckless abandon in the profound darkness.

7 MONDUMÉ WITH PERCUSSION

In the wee hours of the morning, when everyone had retired after a night of *boyobi,* Mabuti sat up and strummed on his *mondumé,* serenading our forest camp until shortly before dawn. He was joined on the stick percussion by Mitumbi and Mosio. Mabuti sings that one must not follow the path of jealousy, for it makes the heart evil.

8 & 9 BOYOBI (PARTS THREE AND FOUR)

These two tracks are taken from a final night of the *boyobi* presented earlier. For more than a week afterward no more *boyobi* was sung, and the Bayaka shifted their interest to *gano* (the sung and spoken fables, mostly performed by men) and *yeyi*. Only when they moved camp did *boyobi* again become paramount. The first song is a lovely rendition of what one might call the "main melody" of the Bayaka's three-month forest sojourn. The melody, introduced by the *bobé* during a *boyobi* that took place in the first major camp away from the village, is actually a very old one. Over the next three months the women explored every aspect of this melody, altering its rhythm, developing counter-melodies from it, changing the emphasis of its notes so that its beginning and end became the middle of a seemingly new melody. Sometimes a night of *boyobi* consisted entirely of variations of this single melody.

The second track begins with the falsetto screeches and rapid speech of the *bobé*, who demanded that the women keep singing, for the *bobé's* energy for dancing had yet to be exhausted, even if the women themselves are ready to sleep. Toward the end, the melodic singing is abandoned and rhythmic cries take over: this part of the *boyobi* is called *esimé* and customarily follows each song. During the *esimé* the dancing of the *bobé* (in this case more than ten phosphorescent figures) can become truly spectacular.

77

10 FUNERAL SONG

When a woman has died, and after she has been buried, the women assemble again to sing *limboku.* Their performance is both a farewell to the woman, and a reestablishing of the natural and harmonious relationship between community and cosmos. If many women are away at the time of such a *limboku* (for example, off in distant forest camps), a second *limboku* will sometimes be performed when they return and are all together. In this *limboku,* recorded at Amapolo in 1987, the occasion was the death of an old woman. About forty women were involved. The voice of the spirit *limboku* is clearly audible. The middle section contains phrases like "she is sleeping" and "no more hunting." In the final section, the women are chanting "she calls *limboku.*"

11 WOMEN OFF TO GATHER PAYU

Shortly after dawn a group of five women set out from our forest camp to collect *payu.* The women sang *yeyi* songs as they went. I recorded them until their gorgeous voices were absorbed by the other sounds of the forest. It was a typical scene of life among the Bayaka, for the women are always singing as the go off into the forest, whether to fetch water at a stream, to join the men on a net hunt or to gather *koko* and mushrooms. Frequent as such moments are, their poignancy never fails to move me. Isn't the forest lonelier without them?

LOUIS SARNO

I would like to acknowledge a decade of assistance from the James A. Swan Fund of the Pitt Rivers Museum in Oxford, England, without which many of these recordings of Bayaka music and forest would never have been made.

[With over fifty albums to his name, Dr. Bernie Krause has been recording wildlife and natural sounds since 1968. He is the President and Director of Wild Sanctuary, which specializes in terrestrial and marine bio-acoustic recording and analysis, museum exhibit sound sculpture design and the creation of music and effects for electronic media.]

During the early spring of 1994, after several years of correspondence, I finally had the opportunity to meet with Louis Sarno in London. I had read about his work and had even bought a few early tape cassettes he had made of the BaBenzélé that, at the time, he diligently copied one by one and sold by mail. Once his astounding recordings began to unfold on my sound system it became clear I was experiencing the field work of a rare genius. I thought, "What a wonderful contribution this man has made bringing this material out of the forests of central Africa." I have been recording natural sounds in the forests and oceans of the world since the end of the 60s and have become familiar with most of those attempting to do work similar to that of Sarno. However, the recordings of the indigenous group with which he has lived, worked and hunted for the past decade demonstrates a special level of devotion and connection that many of the other recordists lacked. At one point in our exchange of letters, he observed that the music of the Bayaka seemed to evolve from the sounds of the natural environment, exactly what I had first recognized while working in Africa in 1983. I knew immediately that we had been sharing a rare experience in common without ever expressing the significance of our discovery.

As it happened, I had been thinking of the ways in which natural sound might have influenced our ancient music for quite a while. Inspired by a friend who lived on the Nez Perce Indian reservation in Idaho, I began to hear music around me as being linked very closely to the sounds of the natural environment. In fact, the closer the connection, the more attractive and compelling the music became for me. To demonstrate the point, one cold October 1971 morning, Angus Wilson took me to a place sacred to his Native American group and made me listen to the wind whistling through the reeds by a small stream. The effect ranged from the sound of a great church pipe organ with all stops pulled out to a simple pan pipe flute depending on the force of the wind at any given moment. Later, during his demonstration, Wilson cut a length of reed from among the many that grew along the shore, and bored requisite holes for the flute he was to subsequently play on one of my albums. His contribution became a major component of the strongest piece on the record.

A little later in the decade, R. Murry Schafer, the Canadian philosopher and sound sculptor, added fuel to the fire of discovery when he suggested that sound in any environment provides meaningful clues as to "the effects of the acoustic environment...or the physical responses or behavioral characteristics of those living within it." Just what were these clues?

No matter how strong the evidence that music grew out of a larger context, during the period of my Western undergraduate education, I was largely taught to ignore any indications. Eurocentric visions of music pervaded much of what we were offered then, both in the marketplace and academia. At the time, little serious attention was paid to emerging influences coming from Africa, Asia, India and Latin America (even though some had been well-represented in North America for nearly two hundred years by the middle of the 20th century). So far had we drifted from our ancient roots that even the strongest intimation of the connection was pretty much disregarded. In large part, I suspect this is because we had no particular interest in tracing this odd-sounding music back to its point of origin since we were so involved in our own limited creations. To suggest that music was nature-related seemed to border on the absurd. After all, nature was something to be conquered and dominated; not studied for its influence on our musical culture. Basically, we had learned to be terrified of "nature." Those who lived in harmony with it and by it were considered to be primitive, or developing, or just plain ignorant. Also, by opening up the study of these possibilities, a new conundrum was posed: The subject was extremely complicated and perplexing for students in the field because very little information could be codified or measured – the heart and soul of any Western academic study. As we have become a culture of specialists, we have lost the ability to see the total picture and our place within it.

As it turns out, these "primitives" have a lexicon of musical expression far more complex, dramatic and dynamic than anything yet posited in the most avant garde of our institutions. I might add, it is an expression much closer to the heart and soul of humanity than anything I've yet to hear coming from late

20th century technologies. Basically, the sounds of primary growth forest environments have taken a very long time to evolve so that each creature can be heard. In any given habitat, birds have their niche, insects have theirs. So do frogs, mammals and reptiles. Not only do these creatures find a place in the system relative to frequency (pitch), but they also find a place for rhythm or a time to be heard when others in their frequency niche are silent. The relationships between the animals themselves and their given environments is sacrosanct. It can now be identified in the deserts, oceans, mountains and every rainforest (temperate, tropical, and sub-Arctic) habitat on the planet. I would describe this phenomenon as a virtual animal orchestra. So well defined are these occurrences that when spectrograms are derived from the creature voices, they can be read and played just as one would utilize a piece of sheet music.

For those living in the rainforests of the world, this creature ambiance has served as their major communication influence. Their radio. Their TV. Their CD and Walkman cassette. Many use these sounds as an animal karaoke orchestra to which they perform. The rhythms from chimps pounding on the buttresses of fig trees have inspired the drum. Frogs rhythms in different habitats have spurred the use of complex time (rhythm) patterns. Lead melody lines have been influenced by bird song and certain mammals. The idea of orchestration itself, comes directly from whole habitats and the way in which creatures perform at different times of the day and night, under different weather conditions and seasons.

The reason Louis Sarno's work is so important is because it conveys, for the first time, the connection between the rainforest, its sounds and the music created by those intimately joined to all of its resources. The best example of this link is "Boyobi at Spear-Hunting Camp (part one)." I should add that because existing recording technologies obviate the ability of recordists to record both music and ambiance at the same time with great success, the music and field recordings had to be done separately and then recombined during the mix. However, they are faithful to the environment and the niche concept.

Finally, my natural sound library consists of nearly 2,700 hours of material from most major habitats around the globe. Nearly twenty percent of that material comes from habitats which are now extinct. Untouched primary environments have become extremely hard to find. As they continue to disappear, we are losing the living resources they provide as well as the valuable knowledge about our musical origins that both the creatures and humans living there might impart to us. The study of single animal voices simply limits us to measurable signals, something safe in academic circles, but containing no useful information that reveals more beneficial secrets. These revelations can only come from lyrical speculation about how creature voices interact with one another – in discovering how the bird song fits with other creatures in its realm. To those, like the Bayaka, the answers are as natural as the air they breath. To us, these issues will remain great mysteries to be unraveled only when we shed the pretenses of our civilization and begin to look far beyond the constraints of what we're supposed to know.

credits

SPECIAL THANKS TO
the staffs of Ellipsis Arts... and Wild Sanctuary and to Annick Lussiez and Sara Driver whose help made this project possible.

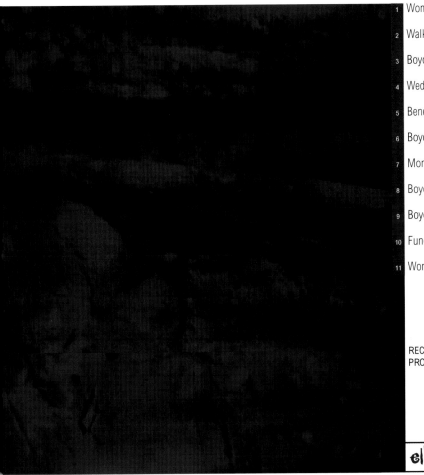

1 Women Gathering Mushrooms 5:13

2 Walking Song 5:17

3 Boyobi at Spear-Hunting Camp (PART ONE) 5:52

4 Wedding Song 3:41

5 Benediction on a Settlement 8:00

6 Boyobi (PART TWO) 5:30

7 Mondumé with Percussion 2:55

8 Boyobi (PART THREE) 6:00

9 Boyobi (PART FOUR) 6:46

10 Funeral Song 4:40

11 Women off to Gather Payu 3:48

RECORDED BY LOUIS SARNO IN CENTRAL AFRICA
PRODUCED AND REMIXED BY BERNIE KRAUSE AT WILD SANCTUARY

ellipsis arts •••

bayaka